COLLECTED POEMS

COLLECTED POEMS

PAUL AUSTER

THE OVERLOOK PRESS
WOODSTOCK & NEW YORK

First published in the United States in 2004 by
The Overlook Press, Peter Mayer Publishers, Inc.
Woodstock & New York

WOODSTOCK:
One Overlook Drive
Woodstock, NY 12498
www.overlookpress.com
[for individual orders, bulk and special sales, contact our Woodstock office]

NEW YORK:
141 Wooster Street
New York, NY 10012

Collection copyright © 2004 by Paul Auster
Introduction © Norman Finkelstein, 2004
Cover painting by Sam Messer

The poems in this book have been taken from the following collections and anthologies: *Unearth* (Living Hand, 1974), *Wall Writing* (The Figures, 1976), *Effigies* (Orange Export Ltd., 1977), *Fragments from Cold* (Parenthèse, 1977), *Facing the Music* (Station Hill, 1980), *White Spaces* (Station Hill, 1980), *A Little Anthology of Surrealist Poems* (Siamese Banana Press, 1972), *The Random House Book of Twentieth-Century French Poetry* (Random House, 1982), *René Char: Selected Poems* (New Directions, 1992). *Spokes* originally appeared in *Poetry* (March 1972).

Grateful acknowledgment is made to the following for permission to include the translations in this book: Editions Gallmard for the poems by Paul Éluard, André Breton, Robert Desnos, Tristan Tzara, and Jacques Dupin; Librarie José Corti for the poems by René Char; Mercure de France for the poems by André du Bouchet; and the Estate of Philippe Soupault.

∞ The paper used in this book meets the requirements for paper
permanence as described in the ANSI Z39.48-1992 standard.

Cataloging-in-Publication Data is available from the Library of Congress

Book design and type formatting by Bernard Schleifer
Manufactured in the United States of America
FIRST EDITION
ISBN 1-58567-404-4
1 3 5 7 9 8 6 4 2

Contents

Introduction

L ONG BEFORE Paul Auster used "the music of chance" as the title to one of his novels, his work was already the embodiment of that phrase. Throughout his career, his writing has been set to that music but simultaneously opposed to it: an ecstatic, frightening investigation of chance and a resistance to its power. How much credit should we give to coincidence? And if we refuse to give it credit, is a belief in determinism our only alternative? And how would a writer make a music out of that? For many years now, Auster's work has happily wandered between the poles of these beliefs, saved from the merely philosophical by the confidence, grace, and sly timing of the born storyteller. Auster has succeeded so brilliantly in giving life to this heady debate—and in doing so, has given us some of the most compelling fiction of our time—because chance, and its equally daunting alternative, fate, have not just been themes that he has chosen to engage in his novels. Rather, as he attests in his interviews and autobiographical works, chance and fate have had everything to do with the literal course of his career, much more so than in the cases of most other writers. And this is especially true regarding his passage from poet to novelist.

As he relates in *Hand to Mouth*, Auster was already trying to write fiction as a teenager, but much of his literary effort during what we would usually consider a writer's formative years, his twenties, went into what we now have before us as his *Collected Poems*. Between 1974 and 1980 he published six collections and chapbooks, a substantial and highly original body of work. Influenced by a select group of precursors, both American (Dickinson, Reznikoff, Oppen, Olson) and continental (Celan, Mandelstam, the French Surrealists), it is a poetry that develops rapidly, following a trajectory from taut and furious to open and reconciled, from the reduced minims of world and language to generous valediction.

But it ends, it definitively ends. As he reports in an extraordinary interview with Larry McCaffery and Sinda Gregory (in *The Art of Hunger*), by 1978, with a failing marriage, a young child, and desperate money problems, Auster had virtually stopped writing. Then, in December, Auster chanced to attend the rehearsal of a dance piece choreographed by a friend of a friend. The piece so inspired him that he began to write *White Spaces*, "a little work," as he puts it, "of no identifiable genre—which was an attempt on my part to translate the experience of that dance performance into words. It was a liberation for me, a tremendous letting go, and I look back on it now as the bridge between writing poetry and writing prose." But that's not all. *White Spaces* was finished late on the night of January 14th 1979. ("A few scraps of paper. A last cigarette before turning in. The snow falling endlessly in the winter night. To remain in the realm of the naked eye, as happy as I am at this moment.") Early the next morning, Auster learned of his father's sudden death the night before. The inheritance he received temporarily freed him from financial concerns and gave him the time he needed to work on the prose he believed he had permanently abandoned. He turned to writing *The Invention of Solitude*—a monument, as he told me, to his first life—and from there went on to *The New York Trilogy*, sections of which, along with parts of In *the Country of Last Things* and *Moon Palace*, had actually been germinating for many years.

Was it chance or fate that led Auster to that dance rehearsal, from which came the uncanny liberation of *White Spaces?* Was it coincidence that the work should be finished even as his father died? And in the light of these events, this classic Auster story of a strange shift from one phase of a life to the next, how are we to read his poems? "I remain very attached to the poetry I wrote," says Auster in the same interview. "I still stand by it. In the final analysis, it could even be the best work I've ever done." Indeed, these are haunting, challenging poems, to which I for one have returned continually, even as I have anticipated and devoured each of Auster's novels in turn. Auster fans (yes, this is a writer not only with readers but with fans) will have at least read the poetry in *Disappearances;* they will be pleased to see all the poems now gathered here, along with a selection of Auster's revealing translations. Those who are just beginning to enter his world, having perhaps read a novel or two, are urged to pause and consider his world through his poems, for as Auster says, "poetry is like taking still photographs, whereas prose is like filming with a movie camera." And the serious readers of poetry—the audience that I continually seek, as both poet and critic—should pay particular attention to this book, should read it thoughtfully, read it with pleasure, and contemplate it in relation to the larger poetic landscape of our time.

II

"The world is in my head. My body is in the world."
—*Notes From A Composition Book* (1967)

THE TWENTY YEAR OLD who writes this proposition, immersed in Wittgenstein, Merleau-Ponty, and the prose of Charles Olson, will soon go on to produce what might at first appear to be a dauntingly abstract poetry. But like Olson (as in "In Cold Hell, In Thicket" and "As the Dead Prey Upon Us"), and in a related key, like the Objectivists, Auster struggles toward the real, and his poetry enacts that process. He reaches from the world in his head to the world that he knows his body inhabits, with language, as he realizes, as his only "means of organizing experience." "The eye sees the world in flux," writes this student of perception; "The word is an attempt to arrest the flow, to stabilize it. And yet we persist in trying to translate experience into language. Hence poetry, hence the utterances of daily life. This is the faith that prevents universal despair—and also causes it." As Auster already recognizes (and I think this is a key to both his poetry and his fiction), there is a fundamental kinship between poetic and mundane utterance, which leads me to question our initial sense of the poetry's abstract intensities.

Item: the Auster home in New Jersey where Paul spent his teenage years—and where his parents' marriage gradually collapsed—was located so close to a quarry that he could regularly hear the blasts ("Picks jot the quarry—eroded marks / That could not cipher the message. / The quarrel unleashed its alphabet, / And the stones, girded by abuse / Have memorized the defeat"). Item: many of the poems were written among the rocky landscapes of the south of France, where, as he relates in *The Red Notebook,* Auster and his companion nearly starved, working as caretakers of a farmhouse owned by an American couple in Paris ("Night-light: the bone and the breath / transparent"). Item: Auster attends Columbia University during the chaotic upheavals of be late sixties. The suspicion of authority, the politics of rage, produce what Auster tells me is the "radical anarchist subtext" of *Unearth* ("with imbecilic hands, they dragged you / into the city, bound you in / this knot of slang, and gave you / nothing. Your ink has learned / the violence of the wall"). Item: a few years later, with the storm of Watergate gathering just ahead, he watches the election results with other Americans in our embassy in Paris as Nixon is reelected in the biggest landslide in U. S. history. Appalled, Auster writes "Lies. Decrees. 1972." ("Imagine: / even now / he does not repent of / his oath, even / now, he stammers back, unwitnessed, to his / resurrected throne").

So the stony interior world is surprisingly congruent with the equally stony exterior world. The strange meetings with an other which inspire poem after poem are less encounters with

Romantic doppelgängers and femmes fatales than they are the accounts of a restless young man, formidably intelligent, who is determined to make lasting contact with the world outside his own head. Sometimes the "you" is a lover; sometimes it may be himself. Sometimes it is a literary relation, as in the address to Celan in "White" or to Mandelstam in "Siberian." But in every instance, the urgency of the communication, combined with an innate respect (honor *and* fear) of language, is such that he finds himself, as he declares at the end of "Lapsarian," "standing in the place / where the eye most terribly holds / its ground." Indeed, as the poetry nears its end, in a piece called, appropriately, "Quarry," it is "The world / that walks inside me" that has become "a world beyond reach." As Auster seeks the embrace of the outside world, maintaining lyric interiority increasingly becomes the problem. The poems, as he tells McCaffery and Gregory, "were a quest for what I would call a uni-vocal expression. . . . They were concerned with bedrock beliefs, and their aim was to achieve a purity and consistency of language. Prose, on the other hand, gives me a chance to articulate my conflicts and contradictions." Thus, one of our most "French" of recent poets, with his Mallarméan designs on linguistic purity, gives way to the novelist's dialogic imagination. And as Auster confirms, "Of all the theories of the novel, Bakhtin's strikes me as the most brilliant, the one that comes closest to understanding the complexity and the magic of the form."

In hindsight, this may provide a clue to the title of Auster's last collection, *Facing the Music.* Something is shutting down, something is opening up in these memorable poems; the sense of change is palpable. The first lines of "Narrative" read like the beginning of one of the early novels ("Because what happens will never happen, / and because what has happened / endlessly happens again . . ."). The father is mourned with the utmost self-consciousness ("As if the first word / comes only after the last . . ."); a few pages later comes a Beckett-like elegy to the self ("Simply to have stopped"). Or perhaps it is the *poetic* self. In "Search for a Definition," the speaker declares that it

> will never become
> a question
> of trying to simplify
> the world, but a way of looking for a place
> to enter the world, a way of being
> present
> among the things
> that do not want us . . .

As these lines indicate, by this point Auster has learned the lessons of the Objectivists, especially those of George Oppen, very well indeed. But rather than attempt a genuinely dialogic lyric sequence like *Of Being Numerous*, he moves instead toward the "elsewhere" of narrative prose. Hence what I feel to be the tremendous pathos of "Facing the Music," a valediction to poetry rarely found in modern letters:

> Impossible
> to hear it anymore. The tongue
> is forever taking us away
> from where we are, and nowhere
> can we be at rest
> in the things we are given
> to see, for each word
> is an elsewhere, a thing that moves more
> quickly than the eye . . .

III

I T IS DIFFICULT FOR ME to separate my reading of these poems with my own start as a poet. I first encountered Auster's work in 1976, in a little magazine called *The Mysterious Barricades*, edited by Henry Weinfield, the poet, critic, and translator who was my first creative writing teacher. Henry had accepted three of my poems for publication. It was the first appearance of my work outside of a student magazine, and I read the issue from cover to cover, including Auster's five poems from *Wall Writing*, which would appear that same year. Auster's poems were among the most compelling, along with the eight poems of William Bronk, to whose work I had already been exposed, and those of Weinfield himself. I remember looking up the word "viaticum" and learning of its specific Catholic sense ("the Eucharist, as given to a dying person or one in danger of death") as well as its more general meaning ("supplies for a journey"). Auster had used it as the title of a poem that I found perfectly balanced between terror and compassion. I was equally moved by "White," which I would only later understand was in memory of Celan, and by "Ascendant," with its powerfully confident appropriations of Jewish tradition ("The sabbath candle / torn from your throat"). Here was a poet, I thought, with both an unusual reach and a sharply focused style. I got hold of as many of his books as I could find.

It took me until 1979 to write to Auster. By then, I was soliciting work for *Daimon,* a magazine I co-edited with other members of a shortlived but energetic group of young writers that called itself the Atlanta Poetry Collective. He graciously sent me what remains one of my favorites among his poems, the electrifying midrash on the biblical figure of Jacob called "Between the Lines." Ironically, *Daimon* folded before we could publish the poem, but the condensed, incantatory lines stayed with me, and nearly twenty years later, I would borrow three of them ("to the seventh year / beyond the seventh year / of the seventh year") for a long movement of my serial poem *Track,* a movement in seven sections of seven lyrics each, each lyric consisting of seven lines—a movement, of course, about luck and chance.

In the interim, Paul and I continued to correspond; we met in New York on several occasions; and in 1986, he came to Cincinnati to read at Xavier. When *Disappearances* was published, I wrote an essay on the poetry, one of the only sustained examinations of this crucial part of the Auster oeuvre. (It can be found in *Beyond the Red Notebook: Essays on Paul Auster*, edited by Dennis Barone.) Years went by, and we lost touch. One day in April of this year, a book arrived in the mail: *Paul Auster endeckt Charles Reznikoff*, a volume of Reznikoff's poetry selected by Auster and translated into German ("Wie Saloman / habe ich die Sprache von Fremden geheiratet und geheiratet; / keine ist wie du, Sulamit"). I opened the book and found this note:

> Norman—
>
> Years and years . . . In a lovely twist, it was Michael Palmer who sent me your current address.
>
> Reznikoff in German. I thought you might like to have a copy—and send it to you with all good and happy memories of those days we spent together long ago.
>
> Yrs. ever—
>
> Paul A.

It was yet another coincidence, as my own book on Jewish American poetry, including a number of chapters on Reznikoff, had appeared less than a year before. My initial interest in Reznikoff had been prompted by "The Decisive Moment," Auster's early essay on his poetry, and I had returned to it as I thought through my own position on that deceptively simple work. And so, brought together by old affections, our friendship resumed.

That Auster, among the many perceptive writers of his generation, should have been one of the earliest and keenest readers of Reznikoff and the other Objectivists, does not surprise me. Likewise his appreciation for Laura Riding, for William Bronk, for Celan, for Jabès, and of course, for Beckett. Thinking now about Auster's poetry in the light of his essays in *The Art of Hunger*, and in the light of this poetry's own unique history, I understand that it is constituted of a solitary voice speaking to the silence. It is a silence that itself has a complex history, often connected to some of the most terrible episodes in modern times. In the end, it takes up residence within the poet and demands to be acknowledged. I believe we hear Auster addressing the silence in "Testimony," when he speaks of

> . . . how I might acquit you
> of this hiddenness, and prove to you
> that I am
> no longer alone,
> that I am not
> even near myself
> anymore.

As he draws his readers to him, he is indeed no longer alone. And however isolated the voice in these poems may sound, we too are no longer alone when we are near them.

—NORMAN FINKELSTEIN
Cincinnati, Ohio 2003

SPOKES
1970

1

Roots writhe with the worm—the sift
Of the clock cohabits the sparrow's heart.
Between branch and spire—the word
Belittles its nest, and the seed, rocked
By simpler confines, will not confess.
Only the egg gravitates.

2

In water—my absence in aridity. A flower.
A flower that defines the air.
In the deepest well, your body is fuse.

3

The bark is not enough. It furls
Redundant shards, will barter
Rock for sap, blood for veering sluice,
While the leaf is pecked, brindled
With air, and how much more, furrowed
Or wrapped, between dog and wolf,
How much longer will it stake
The axe to its gloating advantage?

4

Nothing waters the bole, the stone wastes nothing.
Speech could not cobble the swamp,
And so you dance for a brighter silence.
Light severs wave, sinks, camouflages—
The wind clacks, is bolt.
I name you desert.

5

Picks jot the quarry—eroded marks
That could not cipher the message.
The quarrel unleashed its alphabet,
And the stones, girded by abuse,
Have memorized the defeat.

6

Drunk, whiteness hoards its strength,
When you sleep, sun drunk, like a seed
That holds its breath
Beneath the soil. To dream in heat
All heat
That infests the equilibrium
Of a hand, that germinates
The miracle of dryness. . .
In each place you have left
Wolves are maddened
By the leaves that will not speak.
To die. To welcome red wolves
Scratching at the gates: howling
Page—or you sleep, and the sun
Will never be finished.
It is green where black seeds breathe.

7

The flower is red, is perched
Where roots split, in the gnarl
Of a tower, sucking in its meager fast,
And retracting the spell
That welds step to word
And ties the tongue to its faults.
The flower will be red
When the first word tears the page,
Will thrive in the ooze, take color,
Of a lesioned beak, when the sparrow
Is bloodied, and flies from one
Earth into the bell.

8

Between the sparrow and the bird without name:
its prey.

Light escapes through the interval.

9

Each trance pales in the hub, the furtive
Equinox of names: pawl
Thwarting ratchet—jarring skies that orb
This austere commerce with wind.
Lulls mend. But gales nourish
Chance: breath, blooming, while the wheel scores
Its writing into earth. Bound back
To your feet. Eyes tend soil
In the cool of dying suns. The song
Is in the step.

10

Embering to the lip
Of nether sky—the undevoured nest-light
Ebbs to sustenance: from the sparrow
To the bird without name, the interval
Is prey—smoke
That softens coals, unlike the sect
Of wings, where you beat, smoke wed
To glow—in the sparrow's memory
It perfects the sleep of clouds.

11

To see is this other torture, atoned for
In the pain of being seen: the spoken,
The seen, contained in the refusal
To speak, and the seed of a single voice,
Buried in a random stone.
My lies have never belonged to me.

12

Into the hub the shell implodes,
Endures as a pun of loam and rock,
Rising as stick, to invade, to drive
Out the babble that worded its body
To emerge, to wait for future
Blows—city in root, in deed, unsprung, even out
Of the city. Get out. The wheel
Was deception. It cannot turn.

13

The egg limits renunciation, cannot
Sound in another's ringing, the least
Hammering, before the wail slits
Its course, and the eye squanders
The subterfuge of a longer lamp.
Lifted into speech, it carries
Its own birth, and if it shatters
Acclaim its fall and contradiction.
Your earth will always be far.

UNEARTH
1970–1972

1

Along with your ashes, the barely
written ones, obliterating
the ode, the incited roots, the alien
eye—with imbecilic hands, they dragged you
into the city, bound you in
this knot of slang, and gave you
nothing. Your ink has learned
the violence of the wall. Banished,
but always to the heart
of brothering quiet, you cant the stones
of unseen earth, and smooth your place
among the wolves. Each syllable
is the work of sabotage.

2

Flails, the whiteness, the flowers
of the promised land: and all
you hoard, crumbling at the brink
of breath. For a single word
in air we have not breathed, for one
stone, splitting with the famine
inside us—ire,
out of bone's havoc, by which we kin
the worm. The wall
is your only witness. Barred
from me, but squandering nothing,
you sprawl over each unwritten page,
as though your voice had crawled
from you: and entered the whiteness
of the wail.

3

The blind way is etched
in your palm: it leads to the voice
you had bartered, and will bleed, once again
on the prongs of this sleep-hewn
braille. A breath
scales the wick of my stammering,
and lights the air that will never
recant. Your body is your own
measured burden. And walks with the weight
of fire.

4

Vatic lips, weaned
of image. The mute one
here, who waits, urn-wise,
in wonder. Curse overbrims
prediction: the glacial rose
bequeaths its thorns to the breath
that labors toward eye
and oblivion.
We have only to ready ourselves.
From the first step, our voice
is in league
with the stones of the field.

5

Night, as though tasted
within. And of us, each lie
the tongue would know
when it draws back and sinks
into its poison.
We would sleep, side by side
with such hunger, and from the fruit
we war with, become the name
of what we name. As though a crime, dreamed
by us, could ripen in cold—and fell
these black, roweling trees
that drain the history of stars.

6

Unquelled
in this flood of earth—
where seeds end
and augur nearness—you will sound
the choral rant
of memory, and go the way
that eyes go. There is no longer
path for you: from the moment
you slit your veins, roots will begin
to recite the massacre
of stones. You will live. You will build
your house here—you will forget
your name. Earth
is the only exile.

7

Thistle, drenched by heat,
and the barren word
that prods you—shouted
down to the lodes.
Light would spill here.
It would seep through
the scrawled branch that wrote
such cowering above us.
As if, far from you,
I could feel it breaking
through me, as I walked
north into my body.

8

Scanned by no one
but the loved, the margins
rehearse your death,
playing out the travesty
of nakedness, and the hands
of all the others
who will see you, as if, one day,
you would sing to them, and in the longer
silence of the anvil, name them
as you would this sun: a stone,
scourged by sky.

9

Between these spasms
of light, in brittle fern, in dark
thickets: waiting
in your labyrinthine ear
for the thunder
to crack: for the Babel-roar,
for the silence. It will not
be what you wandered to
that is heard. But the step,
burrowing under
this parted sky, that keeps its distance
whole. And that widens in you
at the mouth
of cloven earth, where you watch
these fallen stars
struggle to crawl back to you,
bearing the gifts of hell.

10

Ice—means nothing
is miracle, if it must
be what will—you are the means
and the wound—opening
out of ice, and the cadence through
blunt earth, when crows
come to maraud. Wherever you walk, green
speaks into you, and holds. Silence
stands the winter eye to eye
with spring.

11

Scrolls of your second earth, unraveled
by my slow, incendiary hands.
The sky in your name—sliding down
scarps of blueness: the sky
overroaring wheat.
Do not ask—for what. Say nothing—
watch. Parades of the beaten,
for whom I tore apart
the drum. Your other life, glowing in the fuse
of this one. The unbaked loaves: the retina's lack
of solace.

12

Wind-spewn, from the radiant
no, and grafted on
the brown-green scar of this
moment. You ask
what place this is, and I, along the seams
of your dismembering,
have told you: the forest
is the memory
of itself, this frail
splinter, streaming through
my navigable blood and driven
aground in heart-rubble. You ask
words of me, and I
will speak them—from the moment
I have learned
to give you nothing.

13

Other of I: or sibling
axe of shadow, born bright
where fear is darkest—I breathe
to become your whetstone.
Rasping, as of sparks
that keen, as from mire, waves
of sedge that bristle upward
in the hot morning—we would grow
to become part
of such things. Invisible
at last, as this blood is, buried
under loss that knit
to scars. As the unaborted
who will breathe with us,
standing in the glare
of this lewd and figment sun.

14

From one stone touched
to the next stone
named: earth-hood: the inaccessible
ember. You
will sleep here, a voice
moored to stone, moving through
this empty house that listens
to the fire that destroyed it. You
will begin. To drag your body
from the ashes. To carry the burden
of eyes.

15

River-noises, cool. A remnant
grief, merging
with the not yet nameable.
Barge wake, silt, and autumn. Head-
waters churn, a strand
of kelp
wheels over the rank
whey of foam—as one, nail-pierced
shard, twice, floats past you, salvaging
asylum
in eyes washed clean
of bliss.

16

Prayer-grown—
in the ghost-written tract
of your somewhere,
in the landscape
where you will not stand—whorl-bits
of ammonite
reinvent you.
They roll you along
with earth's mock caroling
underfoot, scattering
the hundred-faced lie
that makes you visible. And from each
daylight blow, your hardness turns
to weapon, another slum
flowers within. (Prayer-grown—
the clandestine word, as though cutting
through the hand
that groped along these cave walls): wherever
I do not find you, the silent
mob that drifted mouthward—throngs
loudly into time.

17

Mirrored by the tent-speech
of our forty-dark, alodial-hued
next year—
the images,
ground in the afterlight
of eyes, the wandered
images absolve you: (dunes
that whirled free,—scree-words
shuttled
by the grate of sand,—the other
glass-round hours, redoubling
in remembrance). And in
my hand—(as, after the night,—the night)—
I hold what you have taken
to give: this path
of tallied cries, and grain
after grain, the never-done-with
desert, burning on your lips
that jell in violence.

18

Frail dawn: the boundary
of your darkened lamp: air
without word: a rose-round, folding
corolla of ash. From the smallest
of your suns, you clench
the scald: husk
of relented light: the true seed
in your fallow palm, deepening
into dumbness. Beyond this hour, the eye
will teach you. The eye will learn
to long.

19

Notched out
on this crust of field—in the day
that comes after us,
where you saw the earth
almost happen again: the echoing
furrows have closed,
and for this one-more-life have ransomed you
against the avid murmur
of scythes. Count me along, then,
with your words. Nothing,
even on this day, will change.
Shoulder to shoulder with dust, before
the blade and beyond
the tall dry grass
that veers with me, I am the air's
stammered relic.

20

Evening, at half-mast
through mulberry-glow and lichen: the banner
of the unpronounceable
future. The skull's
rabble
crept out from you—doubling
across the threshold—and became
your knell
among the many: you
never heard it
again. Anti-stars
above the city you expel
from language, turning, at odds,
even with you, repeal the arson-
eye's quiet
testimony.

21

Rats wake in your sleep
and mime the progress
of want. My voice turns back
to the hunger it gives birth to,
coupling with stones
that jut from red walls: the heart
gnaws, but cannot know
its plunder; the flayed tongue
rasps. We lie
in earth's deepest marrow, and listen
to the breath of angels.
Our bones have been drained.
Wherever night has spoken,
unborn sons prowl the void
between stars.

22

The dead still die: and in them
the living. All space,
and the eyes, hunted
by brittle tools, confined
to their habits.
To breathe is to accept
this lack of air, the only breath,
sought in the fissures
of memory, in the lapse that sunders
this language of feuds, without which earth
would have granted a stronger omen
to level the orchards
of stone. Not even
the silence pursues me.

23

Immune to the craving
gray of fog, hate, uttered
in the eaves, day-
long, kept you near. We
knew that sun
had wormed through the shuttered panes
in drunkenness
only. We knew a deeper void
was being
built by the gulls who scavenged
their own cries. We knew that they
knew the landfall
was mirage.
And was waiting,
from the first hour
I had come to you. My skin,
shuddering in the light.
The light, shattering at my touch.

24

No one's voice, alien
to fall, and once
gathered in the eye that bled
such brightness. Your sinew
does not mend, it is
another rope, braided
by ink, and aching through
this raw hand—that hauls the images
back to us: the clairvoyant
corpse, singing
from his gallows-mirror; a glance,
heavier than stone, hurled
down to April
ice, ringing the bottom
of your breath-well; an eye,
and then
one more. Till vulture
is the word
that gluts this offal, night
will be your prey.

25

Nomad—
till nowhere, blooming
in the prison of your mouth, becomes
wherever you are: you
read the fable
that was written in the eyes
of dice: (it was
the meteor-word, scrawled by light
between us, yet we, in the end,
had no evidence, we
could not produce
the stone). The die-and-the-die
now own your name. As if to say,
wherever you are
the desert is with you. As if,
wherever you move, the desert
is new,
is moving with you.

WALL WRITING
1971–1975

White Nights

No one here,
and the body says: whatever is said
is not to be said. But no one
is a body as well, and what the body says
is heard by no one
but you.

Snowfall and night. The repetition
of a murder
among the trees. The pen
moves across the earth: it no longer knows
what will happen, and the hand that holds it
has disappeared.

Nevertheless, it writes.
It writes: in the beginning,
among the trees, a body came walking
from the night. It writes:
the body's whiteness
is the color of earth. It is earth,
and the earth writes: everything
is the color of silence.

I am no longer here. I have never said
what you say
I have said. And yet, the body is a place
where nothing dies. And each night,
from the silence of the trees, you know
that my voice
comes walking toward you.

Matrix and Dream

Inaudible things, chipped
nightly away:
breath, underground
through winter: well-words
down the quarried light
of lullaby rill
and chasm.

You pass.
Between fear and memory,
the agate
of your footfall turns
crimson
in the dust of childhood.

Thirst: and coma: and leaf—
from the gaps
of the no longer known: the unsigned message,
buried in my body.

The white linen
hanging on the line. The wormwood
crushed
in the field.

The smell of mint
from the ruin.

Interior

Grappled flesh
of the fully other and one.
And each thing here, as if it were the last thing
to be said: the sound of a word
married to death, and the life
that is this force in me
to disappear.

Shutters closed. The dust
of a former self, emptying the space
I do not fill. This light
that grows in the corner of the room,
where the whole of the room
has moved.

Night repeats. A voice that speaks to me
only of smallest things.
Not even things—but their names.
And where no names are—
of stones. The clatter of goats
climbing through the villages
of noon. A scarab
devoured in the sphere
of its own dung. And the violet swarm
of butterflies beyond.

In the impossibility of words,
in the unspoken word
that asphyxiates,
I find myself.

Pulse

This that recedes
will come near to us
on the other side of day.

Autumn: a single leaf
eaten by light: and the green
gaze of green upon us.
Where earth does not stop,
we, too, will become this light,
even as the light
dies
in the shape of a leaf.

Gaping eye
in the hunger of day.
Where we have not been
we will be. A tree
will take root in us
and rise in the light
of our mouths.

The day will stand before us.
The day will follow us
into the day.

Scribe

The name
never left his lips: he talked himself
into another body: he found his room again
in Babel.

It was written.
A flower
falls from his eye
and blooms in a stranger's mouth.
A swallow
rhymes with hunger
and cannot leave its egg.

He invents
the orphan in tatters,

he will hold
a small black flag
riddled with winter.

It is spring,
and below his window
he hears a hundred white stones
turn to raging phlox.

Choral

Whinnied by flint,
in the dream-gait that cantered you across
the clover-swarmed
militant field:

this bit
of earth that inches up
to us again, shattered
by the shrill, fife-sharp tone
that jousts you open, million-fold,
in your utmost
heretic word.

Slowly,
you dip your finger into the wound
from which my voice
escapes.

Meridian

All summer long,
by the gradient rasp-light
of our dark, dune-begetting hands: your stones,
crumbling back to life
around you.

Behind my sheer, raven lid,
one early star,
flushed from a hell of briars,
rears you up, innocent,
towards morning, and peoples your shadow
with names.

Night-rhymed. Harrow-deep.
Near.

Lackawanna

Scree-rails, rust,
remembrance: the no longer bearable, again,
shunting across
your gun-metal earth. The eye
does not will
what enters it: it must always refuse
to refuse.

In the burgeoning frost
of equinox: you will have your name,
and nothing more. Dwarfed
to the reddening seed-space
in which every act
rebuts you, your hot, image-bright pore
again
will force its way

open.

Lies. Decrees. 1972.

Imagine:
the conscripting word
that camped in the squalor
of his fathom-moaned, unapproachable
heaven
goes on warring
in time.

Imagine:
even now
he does not repent of
his oath, even
now, he stammers back, unwitnessed, to his
resurrected throne.

Imagine:
the murdered ones,
cursed and radiant below him,
usher the knives
of their humbled, birth-marked silence, deep
into the alleyways
of his mouth.

Imagine:
I speak this to you,
from the evening of the first day,
undyingly,
along the short, human fuse
of resistance.

Ecliptic. Les Halles.

You were my absence.
Wherever I breathed, you found me
lying in the word
that spoke its way back
to this place.

Silence
was
in the prowled shambles
and marrow
of a cunning, harlot haste—a hunger
that became
a bed for me,

as though the random
Ezekial-wrath
I discovered, the "Live," and the
"yes, he said to us,
when we were in our blood,
Live," had merely been your way
of coming near—

as though somewhere,
visible, an arctic stone, as pale
as semen, had been
dripping, fire-phrase by fire-phrase,
from your lips.

Dictum: After Great Distances

Oleander and rose. The rubble
of earth's other air—where the hummingbird
flies in the shadow
of the hawk. And through each wall, the opening
earth of August,
like a stone that cracks
this wall of sun.

Mountains. And then the lights
of the town
beyond the mountain. The town that lies
on the other side
of light.

We dream
that we do not dream. We wake
in the hours of sleep
and sleep through the silence
that stands over us. Summer
keeps its promise
by breaking it.

Viaticum

You will not blame the stones,
or look to yourself
beyond the stones, and say
you did not long for them
before your face
had turned to stone.
In front of you
and behind you, in the darkness
that moves with day, you almost
will have breathed. And your eyes,
as though your life were nothing more
than a bitter pilgrimage
to this country of want, will open
on the walls
that shut you in your voice,
your other voice, leading you
to the distances of love,
where you lie, closer
to the second
and brighter terror
of living in your death, and speaking
the stone
you will become.

Still Life

Snowfall. And in the nethermost
lode of whiteness,
a memory
that adds your steps
to the lost.

Endlessly,
I would have walked with you.

Fore-Shadows

I breathe you.
I becalm you out of me.
I numb you in the reach
of brethren light.
I suckle you
to the dregs of disaster.

The sky pins a vagrant star
on my chest. I see the wind
as witness, the towering night
that lapsed
in a maze of oaks,
the distance.

I haunt you
to the brink of sorrow.
I milk you of strength.
I defy you,
I deify you
to nothing and
to no one,

I become
your necessary and most violent
heir.

Ireland

Turf-spent, moor-abandoned you,
you, the more naked one, bathed in the dark
of the greenly overrun
deep-glen, of the gray bed
my ghost
pilfered from the mouths
of stones—bestow on me the silence
to shoulder the wings of rooks, allow me
to pass through here again
and breathe the rankly dealt-with air
that still traffics in your shame,
give me the right to destroy you
on the tongue that impales
our harvest, the merciless
acres of cold.

Prism

Earth-time, the stones
tick
in hollows of dust, the arable air
wanders far from home, barbed
wire and road
are erased. Spat
out by the burning
fever in our lungs, the Ur-seed
blooms from crystal, our vermilion breath
refracts us
into many. We will not
ever know ourselves
again. Like the light
that moves between the bars
of light
we sometimes called death,
we, too, will have flowered,
even with such
unquenchable flames
as these.

Wall Writing

Nothing less than nothing.

In the night that comes
from nothing,
for no one in the night
that does not come.

And what stands at the edge of whiteness,
invisible
in the eye of the one who speaks.

Or a word.

Come from nowhere
in the night
of the one who does not come.

Or the whiteness of a word,
scratched
into the wall.

Description of October

The axed, delusion oaks
of our stone warm, celestial north, standing
in the blood-
debted air that grows
around the ripening vineyard. Farther,
even than the drunkenness
we will have breathed,
a magpie wing will turn
and pinion through our shadow.

Come
for the grief pennies
I hold out to you.

Covenant

Throng of eyes,
myriad, at sunken retina depth: the image
of the great, imageless one,
moored within.

Mantis-lunged, we,
the hirelings, alive in juniper and rubble,
broke the flat bread
that went with us, we
were steps, wandered
into blindness, we knew by then
how to breathe ourselves along
to nothing.

Something lost
became
something to be found.
A name,
followed through the dust
of all that veering, did not ever
divulge its sound. The mountain
was the spoor
by which an animal pain
hunted itself home.

All night
I read the braille wounds
on the inner wall
of your cry, and at the brink
of the thick, millennial morning, climbed up
into you again, where all
my bones began
beating and
beating the heart-drum
to shreds.

Shadow to Shadow

Against the facade of evening:
shadows, fire, and silence.
Not even silence, but its fire—
the shadow
cast by a breath.

To enter the silence of this wall,
I must leave myself behind.

Provence: Equinox

Night-light: the bone and the breath
transparent. This journey
of proffered sky
to the core of the sky
we inhabit—a mountain
in the air that crumbles.

You alone
sleep down to the bottom
of this place,
stillborn earth, as though you could dream
far enough
to tell me of the dense, mud-reckoned seed
that burns in us,
and calm the slow, vernal agony
that labors
through the long uprooting
of stars.

Hieroglyph

The language of walls.
Or one last word—
cut
from the visible.

May Day. The metamorphosis
of Solomon's-seal
into stone. The just
doom of the uttered
road, unraveled in the swirl
of pollen-memory
and seed. Do not
emerge, Eden. Stay
in the mouths of the lost
who dream you.

Upon thunder and thorn: the furtive air
arms
the lightning-gorse and silence
of each fallow sky
below. Blood Hebrew. Or what
translates
my body's turning back
to an image of earth.

This knife
I hold against your throat.

White

For one who drowned:
this page, as if
thrown out to sea
in a bottle.

So that
even as the sky embarks
into the seeing of earth, an echo
of the earth
might sail toward him,
filled with a memory of rain,
and the sound of the rain
falling on the water.

So that
he will have learned,
in spite of the wave
now sinking from the crest
of mountains, that forty days
and forty nights
have brought no dove
back to us.

Horizon

You vow yourself away,
you burn yourself
into thaw, you
yellow the cliffs with broom.

My breath
shatters into you. I am
particle
in what heaps you whole,
ash—hovering

in your second sky, in the blue
I hollowed from the blue
of morning.

And the half-said holds
in our frantic lungs, uniting
fire's more with want,
and the word that will carry us
beyond ourselves—

here, where the hard earth
storms toward us, shot through
by wind's reaving awl.

Ascendant

Spun from the hither-word's
most hoarded space of longing,
on the hour and the eve
that evolve
in the web-nonce and never-lattice
of elsewhere-
upon-elsewhere,

you, who groped out
from the ghetto-taut mouth, mother
of mother, through spring's dark
spider havoc
and the first, brute
knowing of ice,

over the bay, and the barges, and the coal
borne outward: diamond
and Jew, and dew-drenched blade
of grass, sundered
by the sharp, heathen sun
in ascent, in sense-
lost Cyrillic—unknowable—
but yours, yes,
and mine,

down to the mica-sheer
parchments, tallying
the living into death again
and life, below, beyond the below, and before,
breath-paved, there, a direction,
yes, and nowhere,
into the real
that was won, and lost, and
re-invented:

The sabbath candle
torn from your throat, burns
through the cold
that would have freed us—I have not
put my weapons aside:

Tundra,
dissolving in the white light
of sleeplessness:

For every pick that breached the quarry,
for each stone
cleft from earth, a star now grows
dim.

South

Hewn till white— : the bronze
heart and heaven-shape
of our gradual
winter.

Do not forget,
my dreamless one, I , too,
came to this world before
the snow.

Pastoral

In the hinterland of moss and waiting,
so little like the word
that was a waiting as well,
all has been other
than it is, the moss
still waits for you, the word
is a lantern
you carry to the depths
of green, for even the roots
have carried light, and even now
your voice
still travels through the roots, so that
wherever an axe may fall
you, too, shall know that you live.

Incendiary

Flint hours. The dumb sprawl
of stones around us, heart
against heart, we, in the straw
hulk
that festers through the damp
lapse of night.

Nothing left. The cold eye
opens on cold,
as an image of fire
eats
through the word
that struggles in your mouth. The world
is
whatever you leave to it, is only
you
in the world my body
enters: this place
where all is lacking.

Song of Degrees

In the vacant lots
of solstice. In the light
you wagered for the rubble
of awe. Sand heaps:
retched into prayer—the distance
bought
in your name.

You. And then
you again. A footstep
gives ground: what is more
is not more: nothing
has ever been
enough. Tents,
pitched and struck: a ladder
propped
on a pillow of stone: the sheer
aureole rungs
of fire. You,
and then we. The earth
does not ask
for anyone.

So
be it. So much
the better—so many
words,
raked and murmured along
by your bedouin knees, will not
conjure you home. Even
if you crawled from the skin
of your brother,

you would not go beyond
what you breathe: no
angel can cure you
of your name.

Minima. Memory
and mirage. In each place
you stop for air,
we will build a city around you. Through the star-
mortared wall
that rises in our night, your soul
will not pass
again.

Fire Speech

You veer out. You crumble in.
You stand.

Cradled
by the hour-gong
that beat through the holly
twelve times
more silent than you, something, let
loose by someone,
rescues your name from coal.

You stand
there again, breathing
in the phantom sun
between ice and reverie.

I have come so far for you,
the voice
that echoes back to me
is no longer my own.

Lapsarian

This bit-open earth.
Arbor: in the neigh of branches.
The shallow night, merging
with noon.

I speak to you
of the word that mires in the smell
of here-after.
I speak to you of the fruit
I shoveled up
from below.
I speak to you of speech.

Humus colors. Buried in the rift
till human. The day's prismatic blessing—divisible
by breath. Starling paths,
snake furrows, seeds. The quick
skewers of flame. What burns
is banished.
Is taken with you.
Is yours.

A man
walks out from the voice
that became me.
He has vanished.
He has eaten
the ripening word
that killed you and
killed you.

He has found himself,
standing in the place
where the eye most terribly holds
its ground.

Late Summer

Borealis flood, and all of night, unleashed
at the eye's diluvian hour. Our bone-
broken will, countering the flow
of stones within our blood: vertigo
from the helium heights
of language.

Tomorrow: a mountain road
lined with gorse. Sunlight
in the fissures of rock. Lessness.
As if we could hold a single breath
to the limit breath.

There is no promised land.

Heraclitian

All earth, accountable
to greenness, the air's ballast
coal, and the winter
that ignites
the fire of earth, as all air moves
unbrokenly
into the green
moment of ourselves. We know that we are
spoken for. And we know that earth
will never yield
a word
small enough to hold us. For the just word
is only of air, and in the green
ember
of our nether sameness, it brings no fear
but that of life. We therefore
will be named
by all that we are not. And whoever
sees himself
in what is not yet
spoken,
will know what it is
to fear
earth
to the just
measure of himself.

Braille

Legibility of earth. Bone's
clear pelt,
and the swerve of plume-and-weal clouds
in victim air—no longer
to be read.

"When you stop on this road,
the road, from that moment on,
will vanish."

And you knew, then,
that there were two of us: you knew
that from all this flesh of air, I
had found the place
where one word
was growing wild.

Nine months darker, my mouth bores through
the bright ways
that cross with yours. Nine lives
deeper, the cry is still
the same.

Salvage

Reunion of ash men
and ash women. Sky's wan hub
grown full till anther-round
on the peat slope from which
I saw them. May-green: what was said,
audible in the eye. The words,
mingled with snow, did not
indict the mouth. I drank
the wine they begrudged me. I stood, perhaps,
beside where you
might have been. I dragged
everything
home to the other world.

Autobiography of the Eye

Invisible things, rooted in cold,
and growing toward this light
that vanishes
into each thing
it illumines. Nothing ends. The hour
returns to the beginning
of the hour in which we breathed: as if
there were nothing. As if I could see
nothing
that is not what it is.

At the limit of summer
and its warmth: blue sky, purple hill.
The distance that survives.
A house, built of air, and the flux
of the air in the air.

Like these stones
that crumble back into earth.
Like the sound of my voice
in your mouth.

All Souls

Anonymity and floe: November
by its only name, death-
danced
through the broken speech
of hoe and furrow
down
from the eaves of overwhelming—these
hammer-worshipped
spew-things
cast
into the zones of blood.

A transfusion of darkness,
the generate peace, encroaching
on slaughter.

Life equal to life.

DISAPPEARANCES
1975

1

Out of solitude, he begins again—

as if it were the last time
that he would breathe,

and therefore it is now

that he breathes for the first time
beyond the grasp
of the singular.

He is alive, and therefore he is nothing
but what drowns in the fathomless hole
of his eye,

and what he sees
is all that he is not: a city

of the undeciphered
event,

and therefore a language of stones,
since he knows that for the whole of life
a stone
will give way to another stone

to make a wall

and that all these stones
will form the monstrous sum

of particulars.

2

It is a wall. And the wall is death.

Illegible
scrawl of discontent, in the image

and after-image of life—

and the many who are here
though never born,
and those who would speak

to give birth to themselves.

He will learn the speech of this place.
And he will learn to hold his tongue.

For this is his nostalgia: a man.

3

To hear the silence
that follows the word of oneself. Murmur

of the least stone

shaped in the image
of earth, and those who would speak
to be nothing

but the voice that speaks them
to the air.

And he will tell
of each thing he sees in this space,
and he will tell it to the very wall
that grows before him:

and for this, too, there will be a voice,
although it will not be his.

Even though he speaks.

And because he speaks.

4

There are the many—and they are here:

and for each stone he counts among them
he excludes himself,

as if he, too, might begin to breathe
for the first time

in the space that separates him
from himself.

For the wall is a word. And there is no word
he does not count
as a stone in the wall.

Therefore, he begins again,
and at each moment he begins to breathe

he feels there has never been another
time—as if for the time that he lived
he might find himself

in each thing he is not.

What he breathes, therefore,
is time, and he knows now
that if he lives

it is only in what lives

and will continue to live
without him.

5

In the face of the wall—

he divines the monstrous
sum of particulars.

It is nothing.
And it is all that he is.
And if he would be nothing, then let him begin
where he finds himself, and like any other man
learn the speech of this place.

For he, too, lives in the silence
that comes before the word
of himself.

6

And of each thing he has seen
he will speak—

the blinding
enumeration of stones,
even to the moment of death—

as if for no other reason
than that he speaks.

Therefore, he says I,
and counts himself
in all that he excludes,

which is nothing,

and because he is nothing
he can speak, which is to say
there is no escape

from the word that is born
in the eye. And whether or not
he would say it,

there is no escape.

7

He is alone. And from the moment he begins to breathe,

he is nowhere. Plural death, born

in the jaws of the singular,

and the word that would build a wall
from the innermost stone
of life.

For each thing that he speaks of
he is not—

and in spite of himself
he says I, as if he, too, would begin
to live in all the others

who are not. For the city is monstrous,
and its mouth suffers
no issue

that does not devour the word
of oneself.

Therefore, there are the many,
and all these many lives
shaped into the stones
of a wall,

and he who would begin to breathe
will learn there is nowhere to go
but here.

Therefore, he begins again,

as if it were the last time
he would breathe.

For there is no more time. And it is the end of time
that begins.

EFFIGIES
1976

1

Eucalyptus roads: a remnant of the pale sky
shuddering in my throat. Through the ballast
drone of summer

the weeds that silence
even your step.

2

The myriad haunts of light.
And each lost thing—a memory

of what has never been. The hills. The impossible
hills

lost in the brilliance of memory.

3

As if it were all

still to be born. Deathless in the eye,
where the eye now opens on the noise

of heat: a wasp, a thistle swaying on the prongs

of barbed wire.

4

You who remain. And you
who are not there. Northernmost word, scattered
in the white

hours of the imageless world—

like a single word

the wind utters and destroys.

5

Alba. The immense, alluvial light. The carillon
of clouds at dawn. And the boats
moored in the jetty fog

are invisible. And if they are there

they are invisible.

FRAGMENTS
FROM COLD
1976–1977

Northern Lights

These are the words
that do not survive the world. And to speak them
is to vanish

into the world. Unapproachable
light
that heaves above the earth, kindling
the brief miracle

of the open eye—

and the day that will spread
like a fire of leaves
through the first chill wind
of October

consuming the world

in the plain speech
of desire.

Reminiscence of Home

True north. Vincent's north.
The glimpsed

unland of light. And through each fissure
of earth, the indigo
fields that burn
in a seething wind of stars.

What is locked
in the eye that possessed you
still serves
as an image of home: the barricade
of an empty chair, and the father, absent,
still blooming in his urn
of honesty.

You will close your eyes.
In the eye of the crow who flies before you,
you will watch yourself
leave yourself behind.

Riding Eastward

A word, unearthed
for Knut Hamsun:

kneaded
on the blood trail back
from America, where the sun-
stoked locomotive roof
baked the consumption
out of him:

with so much distance
to be delved by what is
purely godless, the written
does not damn you
to any fate
worse than self.

You hunger
up the vast bread slopes of feeling,
and begin, breaking once again, your fathomless
alphabet of stones.

Gnomon

September sun, illusionless. The purple
field awash
in the hours of the first breath. You will not
submit to this light, or close your eyes
to the vigilant
crumbling of light in your eyes.

Firmament of fact. And you,
like everything else
that moves. Parsed seed
and thimble of air. Fissured
cloud and worm: the open-
ended sentence that engulfs you
at the moment I begin
to be silent.

Perhaps, then, a world
that secretes its harvest
in the lungs, a means
of survival by breath
alone. And if nothing,
then let nothing be
the shadow
that walks inside your shadow, the body
that will cast
the first stone, so that even as you walk
away from yourself, you might feel it
hunger toward you, hourly,
across the enormous
vineyards of the living.

Fragment from Cold

Because we go blind
in the day that goes out with us,
and because we have seen our breath
cloud
the mirror of air,
the eye of the air will open
on nothing but the word
we renounce: winter
will have been a place
of ripeness.

We who become the dead
of another life than ours.

Aubade

Not even the sky.
But a memory of sky,
and the blue of the earth
in your lungs.

Earth
less earth: to watch
how the sky will enclose you, grow vast
with the words
you leave unsaid—and nothing
will be lost.

I am your distress, the seam
in the wall
that opens to the wind
and its stammering, storm
in the plural—this other name
you give your world: exile
in the rooms of home.

Dawn folds, fathers
witness,
the aspen and the ash
that fall. I come back to you
through this fire, a remnant
of the season to come,
and will be to you
as dust, as air,
as nothing
that will not haunt you.

In the place before breath
we feel our shadows cross.

Testimony

In the high winter wheat
that blew us across
this no man's land,
in the couplings of our anger
below these nameless white weeds,
and because I lodged, everlastingly,
a flower in hell, I tell you
of the opening of my eye
beyond being,
of my being beyond being
only one,
and how I might acquit you
of this hiddenness, and prove to you
that I am
no longer alone,
that I am not
even near myself
anymore.

Visible

Spools of lightning, spun outward
in the split, winter night: thunder
hauled by star—as if

your ghost had passed, burning,
into the needle's eye, and worked itself
sheer though the silk
of nothingness.

Meteor

The light, receding from us once again,
in this furtive, unappeasable
birth
of mineral-memory
and home, as though here,
even our names, anchored
to the glacial prow
of silences, could furrow the land
with longing, and scatter, over the life
that lies between us, the dust
of the smallest stone
that falls from the eaves
of Babel.

Transfusion

Oven's glow. Or vast
hemoglobin
leap—

:the blasphemy
of their death-devoted word, lying
in the self-same blood
your open heart
still squanders.

Pulse—
and then what—(then
what?)—erupts in the skull
of the ghetto sphinx—that plumbs
the filth
and fever of the ones
who gave up. (Like you,
they still hover, still
hunger, immured in the bread
of no one's flesh, still make themselves
felt):

as if, in the distance between
sundown and sunrise,
a hand
had gathered up your soul
and worked it with the stones
into the leaven
of earth.

Siberian

Shadow, carted off by wolves
and quartered, half a life beyond
each barb of the wire, now I see you,
magnetic
polar felon, now I begin
to speak to you
of the wild boar
of southern woods, of scrub
oak and thicket spruce, of thyme-reek
and lavender, even
down to lava, spewn, through each
chink in the wall, so that you, counter-voice, lost
in the cold
of farthest murder, might come
floating back
on your barge of ice, bearing
the untellable
cargo of forgiveness.

Looking Glass

Laid bare
by your rabid, obsidian eye,
by the white
ire and barking
of the mirror-dog who stared you
into blindness:

Spinoza's god,
cast from the borders of speech, geometric,
journeying through the curve
of exile,
hazards another world.

Clandestine

Remember with me today—the word
and counter-word
of witness: the tactile dawn, emerging
from my clenched hand: sun's
ciliary grasp: the stretch of darkness
I wrote
on the table of sleep.

Now
is the time to come.
All you have come
to take from me, take
away from me now. Do not
forget
to forget. Fill
your pockets with earth,
and seal up the mouth
of my cave.

It was there
I dreamed my life
into a dream
of fire.

Quarry

No more than the song of it. As if
the singing alone
had led us back to this place.

We have been here, and we have never been here.
We have been on the way to where we began,
and we have been lost.

There are no boundaries
in the light. And the earth
leaves no word for us
to sing. For the crumbling of the earth
underfoot

is a music in itself, and to walk among these stones
is to hear nothing
but ourselves.

I sing, therefore, of nothing,

as if it were the place
I do not return to—

and if I should return, then count out my life
in these stones: forget
I was ever here. The world
that walks inside me

is a world beyond reach.

FACING THE
MUSIC
1978–1979

Credo

The infinite

tiny things. For once merely to breathe
in the light of the infinite

tiny things
that surround us. Or nothing
can escape

the lure of this darkness, the eye
will discover that we are
only what has made us less
than we are. To say nothing. To say:
our very lives

depend on it.

Obituary in the Present Tense

It is all one to him—
where he begins

and where he ends. Egg white, the white
of his eye: he says
bird milk, sperm

sliding from the word
of himself. For the eye
is evanescent,
clings only to what is, no more here

or less there, but everywhere, every

thing. He memorizes
none of it. Nor does he write

anything down. He abstains
from the heart

of living things. He waits.

And if he begins, he will end,
as if his eye had opened in the mouth

of a bird, as if he had never begun

to be anywhere. He speaks

from distances
no less far than these.

Narrative

Because what happens will never happen,
and because what has happened
endlessly happens again,

we are as we were, everything
has changed in us, if we speak
of the world
it is only to leave the world

unsaid. Early winter: the yellow apples still
unfallen
in a naked tree, the tracks
of invisible deer

in the first snow, and then the snow
that does not stop. We repent
of nothing. As if we could stand
in this light. As if we could stand in the silence
of this single moment

of light.

S. A. 1911-1979

From loss. And from such loss
that marauds the mind—even to the loss

of mind. To begin with this thought: without rhyme

or reason. And then simply to wait. As if the first word
comes only after the last, after a life
of waiting for the word

that was lost. To say no more
than the truth of it: men die, the world fails, the words

have no meaning. And therefore to ask
only for words.

Stone wall. Stone heart. Flesh and blood.

As much as all this.
More.

Search for a Definition

(On Seeing a Painting by Bradley Walker Tomlin)

Always the smallest act

possible
in this time of acts

larger than life, a gesture
toward the thing that passes

almost unseen. A small wind

disturbing a bonfire, for example,
which I found the other day
by accident

on a museum wall. Almost nothing
is there: a few wisps
of white

thrown idly against the pure black
background, no more
than a small gesture
trying to be nothing

more than itself. And yet
it is not here
and to my eyes will never become
a question
of trying to simplify
the world, but a way of looking for a place
to enter the world, a way of being
present
among the things
that do not want us—but which we need
to the same measure that we need
ourselves. Only a moment before
the beautiful

woman
who stood beside me
had been saying how much she wanted
a child
and how time was beginning
to run out on her. We said
we must each write a poem
using the words "a small
wind

disturbing a bonfire." Since that time
nothing

has meant more than the small
act
present in these words, the act
of trying to speak

words

that mean almost nothing. To the very end
I want to be equal

to whatever it is
my eye will bring me, as if
I might finally see myself

let go
in the nearly invisible
things

that carry us along with ourselves and all
the unborn children

into the world.

Between the Lines

Stone-pillowed, the ways
of remoteness. And written in your palm,
the road.

Home, then, is not home
but the distance between
blessed
and unblessed. And whoever puts himself
into the skin
of his brother, will know
what sorrow is
to the seventh year
beyond the seventh year
of the seventh year.

And divide his children in half.

And wrestle in darkness
with an angel.

In Memory of Myself

Simply to have stopped.

As if I could begin
where my voice has stopped, myself
the sound of a word

I cannot speak.

So much silence
to be brought to life
in this pensive flesh, the beating
drum of words
within, so many words

lost in the wide world
within me, and thereby to have known
that in spite of myself

I am here.

As if this were the world.

Bedrock

Dawn as an image
of dawn, and the very sky collapsing
into itself. Irreducible

image
of pure water, the pores of earth
exuding light: such yield

as only light will bring, and the very stones
undead

in the image of themselves.

The consolation of color.

Facing the Music

Blue. And within that blue a feeling
of green, the gray blocks of clouds
buttressed against air, as if
in the idea of rain
the eye
could master the speech
of any given moment

on earth. Call it the sky. And so
to describe
whatever it is
we see, as if it were nothing
but the idea
of something we had lost
within. For we can begin
to remember

the hard earth, the flint
reflecting stars, the undulating
oaks set loose
by the heaving of air, and so down
to the least seed, revealing what grows
above us, as if
because of this blue there could be
this green

that spreads, myriad
and miraculous
in this, the most silent
moment of summer. Seeds
speak of this juncture, define
where the air and the earth erupt
in this profusion of chance, the random

forces of our own lack
of knowing what it is
we see, and merely to speak of it
is to see
how words fail us, how nothing comes right
in the saying of it, not even these words
I am moved to speak
in the name of this blue
and green
that vanish into the air
of summer.

            Impossible
to hear it anymore. The tongue
is forever taking us away
from where we are, and nowhere
can we be at rest
in the things we are given
to see, for each word
is an elsewhere, a thing that moves
more quickly than the eye, even
as this sparrow moves, veering
into the air
in which it has no home. I believe, then,
in nothing

these words might give you, and still
I can feel them
speaking through me, as if
this alone
is what I desire, this blue
and this green, and to say
how this blue
has become for me the essence
of this green, and more than the pure
seeing of it, I want you to feel

this word
that has lived inside me
all day long, this
desire for nothing

but the day itself, and how it has grown
inside my eyes, stronger
than the word it is made of, as if
there could never be another word

that would hold me
without breaking.

WHITE SPACES
1979

Something happens, and from the moment it begins to happen, nothing can ever be the same again.

Something happens. Or else, something does not happen. A body moves. Or else, it does not move. And if it moves, something begins to happen. And even if it does not move, something begins to happen.

It comes from my voice. But that does not mean these words will ever be what happens. It comes and goes. If I happen to be speaking at this moment, it is only because I hope to find a way of going along, of running parallel to everything else that is going along, and so begin to find a way of filling the silence without breaking it.

I ask whoever is listening to this voice to forget the words it is speaking. It is important that no one listen too carefully. I want these words to vanish, so to speak, into the silence they came from, and for nothing to remain but a memory of their presence, a token of the fact that they were once here and are here no longer and that during their brief life they seemed not so much to be saying any particular thing as to be the thing that was happening at the same time a certain body was moving in a certain space, that they moved along with everything else that moved.

Something begins, and already it is no longer the beginning, but something else, propelling us into the heart of the thing that is happening. If we were suddenly to stop and ask ourselves, "Where are we going?", or "Where are we now?", we would be lost, for at each moment we are no longer where we were, but have left ourselves behind, irrevocably, in a past that has no memory, a past endlessly obliterated by a motion that carries us into the present.

It will not do, then, to ask questions. For this is a landscape of random impulse, of knowledge for its own sake—which is to say, a knowledge that exists, that comes into being beyond any possibility of putting it into words. And if just this once we were to abandon ourselves to the supreme indifference of simply being wherever we happen to be, then perhaps we would not be deluding ourselves into thinking that we, too, had at last become a part of it all.

To think of motion not merely as a function of the body but as an extension of the mind. In the same way, to think of speech not as an extension of the mind but as a function of the body. Sounds emerge from the voice to enter the air and surround and bounce off and enter the body that occupies that air, and though they cannot be seen, these sounds are no less a gesture than a hand is when outstretched in the air towards another hand, and in this gesture can be read the entire alphabet of desire, the body's need to be taken beyond itself, even as it dwells in the sphere of its own motion.

On the surface, this motion seems to be random. But such randomness does not, in itself, preclude a meaning. Or if meaning is not quite the word for it, then say the drift, or a consistent sense of what is happening, even as it changes, moment by moment. To describe it in all its details is probably not impossible. But so many words would be needed, so many streams of syllables, sentences, and subordinate clauses, that the words would always lag behind what was happening, and long after all motion had stopped and each of its witnesses had dispersed, the voice describing that motion would still be speaking, alone, heard by no one, deep into the silence and darkness of these four walls. And yet something is happening, and in spite of myself I want to be present inside the space of this moment, of these moments, and to say something, even though it will be forgotten, that will form a part of this journey for the length of the time it endures.

In the realm of the naked eye nothing happens that does not have its beginning and its end. And yet nowhere can we find the place or the moment at which we can say, beyond a shadow of a doubt, that this is where it begins, or this is where it ends. For some of us, it has begun before the beginning, and for others of us it will go on happening after the end. Where to find it? Don't look. Either it is here or it is not here. And whoever tries to find refuge in any one place, in any one moment, will never be where he thinks he is. In other words, say your good-byes. It is never too late. It is always too late.

To say the simplest thing possible. To go no farther than whatever it is I happen to find before me. To begin with this landscape, for example. Or even to note the things that are most near, as if in the tiny world before my eyes I might find an image of the life that exists beyond me, as if in a way I do not fully understand each thing in my life were connected to every other thing, which in turn connected me to the world at large, the endless world that looms up in the mind, as lethal and unknowable as desire itself.

To put it another way. It is sometimes necessary not to name the thing we are talking about. The invisible God of the Hebrews, for example, had an unpronounceable name, and each of the ninety-nine names tradition ascribes to this God was in fact nothing more than a way of acknowledging that-which-cannot-be-spoken, that-which-cannot-be-seen, and that-which-cannot-be-understood. But even on a less exalted plane, in the realm of the visible itself, we often hold back from divulging the thing we are talking about. Consider the word "it." "It" is raining, we say, or how is "it" going? We feel we know what we are saying, and what we mean to say is that it, the word "it," stands for something that need not be said, or something that cannot be said. But if the thing we say is something that eludes us, something we do not understand, how can we persist in saying that we understand what we are saying? And yet it goes without saying that we do.

The "it," for example, in the preceding sentence, "it goes without saying," is in fact nothing less than whatever it is that propels us into the act of speech itself. And if it, the word "it," is what continually recurs in any effort to define it, then it must be accepted as the given, the precondition of the saying of it. It has been said, for example, that words falsify the thing they attempt to say, but even to say "they falsify" is to admit that "they falsify" is true, thus betraying an implicit faith in the power of words to say what they mean to say. And yet, when we speak, we often do not mean to say anything, as in the present case, in which I find these words falling from my mouth and vanishing into the silence they came from. In other words, it says itself, and our mouths are merely the instruments of the saying of it. How does it happen? But never do we ask what "it" happens to be. We know, even if we cannot put it into words. And the feeling that remains within us, the discretion of a knowledge so fully in tune with the world, has no need of whatever it is that might fall from our mouths. Our hearts know what is in them, even if our mouths remain silent. And the world will know what it is, even when nothing remains in our hearts.

A man sets out on a journey to a place he has never been before. Another man comes back. A man comes to a place that has no name, that has no landmarks to tell him where he is. Another man decides to come back. A man writes letters from nowhere, from the white space that has opened up in his mind. The letters are never received. The letters are never sent. Another man sets out on a journey in search of the first man. This second man becomes more and more like the first man, until he, too, is swallowed up by the whiteness. A third man sets out on a journey with no hope of ever getting anywhere. He wanders. He continues to wander. For as long as he remains in the realm of the naked eye, he continues to wander.

I remain in the room in which I am writing this. I put one foot in front of the other. I put one word in front of the other, and for each step I take I add another word, as if for each word to be spoken there were another space to be crossed, a distance to be filled by my body as it moves through this space. It is a journey through space, even if I get nowhere, even if I end up in the same place I started. It is a journey through space, as if into many cities and out of them, as if across deserts, as if to the edge of some imaginary ocean, where each thought drowns in the relentless waves of the real.

I put one foot in front of the other, and then I put the other foot in front of the first, which has now become the other and which will again become the first. I walk within these four walls, and for as long as I am here I can go anywhere I like. I can go from one end of the room to the other and touch any of the four walls, or even all the walls, one after the other, exactly as I like. If the spirit moves me, I can stand in the center of the room. If the spirit moves me in another direction, I can stand in any one of the four corners. Sometimes I touch one of the four corners and in this way bring myself into contact with two walls at the same time. Now and then I let my eyes roam up to the ceiling, and when I am particularly exhausted by my efforts there is always the floor to welcome my body. The light, streaming through the windows, never casts the same shadow twice, and at any given moment I feel myself on the brink of discovering some terrible, unimagined truth. These are moments of great happiness for me.

Somewhere, as if unseen, and yet closer to us than we realize (down the street, for example, or in the next neighborhood), someone is being born. Somewhere else, a car is speeding along an empty highway in the middle of the night. In that same night, a man is hammering a nail into a board. We know nothing about any of this. A seed stirs invisibly in the earth, and we know nothing about it. Flowers wilt, buildings go up, children cry. And yet, for all that, we know nothing.

It happens, and as it continues to happen, we forget where we were when we began. Later, when we have traveled from this moment as far as we have traveled from the beginning, we will forget where we are now. Eventually, we will all go home, and if there are those among us who do not have a home, it is certain, nevertheless, that they will leave this place to go wherever it is they must. If nothing else, life has taught us all this one thing: whoever is here now will not be here later.

I dedicate these words to the things in life I do not understand, to each thing passing away before my eyes. I dedicate these words to the impossibility of finding a word equal to the silence inside me.

In the beginning, I wanted to speak of arms and legs, of jumping up and down, of bodies tumbling and spinning, of enormous journeys through space, of cities, of deserts, of mountain ranges stretching farther than the eye can see. Little by little, however, as these words began to impose themselves on me, the things I wanted to do seemed finally to be of no importance. Reluctantly, I abandoned all my witty stories, all my adventures of far-away places, and began, slowly and painfully, to empty my mind. Now emptiness is all that remains: a space, no matter how small, in which whatever is happening can be allowed to happen.

And no matter how small, each and every possibility remains. Even a motion reduced to an apparent absence of motion. A motion, for example, as minimal as breathing itself, the motion the body makes when inhaling and exhaling air. In a book I once read by Peter Freuchen, the famous Arctic explorer describes being trapped by a blizzard in northern Greenland. Alone, his supplies dwindling, he decided to build an igloo and wait out the storm. Many days passed. Afraid, above all, that he would be attacked by wolves—for he heard them prowling hungrily on the roof of his igloo—he would periodically step outside and sing at the top of his lungs in order to frighten them away. But the wind was blowing fiercely, and no matter how hard he sang, the only thing he could hear was the wind. If this was a serious problem, however, the problem of the igloo itself was much greater. For Freuchen began to notice that the walls of his little shelter were gradually closing in on him. Because of the particular weather conditions outside, his breath was literally freezing to the walls, and with each breath the walls became that much thicker, the igloo became that much smaller, until eventually there was almost no room left for his body. It is surely a frightening thing, to imagine breathing yourself into a coffin of ice, and to my mind considerably more compelling than, say, *The Pit and the Pendulum* by Poe. For in this case it is the man himself who is the agent of his own destruction, and further, the instrument of that destruction is the very thing he needs to keep himself alive. For surely a man cannot live if he does not breathe. But at the same time, he will not live if he does breathe. Curiously, I do not remember how Freuchen managed to escape his predicament. But needless to say, he did escape. The title of the book, if I recall, is *Arctic Adventure*. It has been out of print for many years.

Nothing happens. And still, it is not nothing. To invoke things that have never happened is noble, but how much sweeter to remain in the realm of the naked eye.

It comes down to this: that everything should count, that everything should be a part of it, even the things I do not or cannot understand. The desire, for example, to destroy everything I have written so far. Not from any revulsion at the inadequacy of these words (although that remains a distinct possibility), but rather from the need to remind myself, at each moment, that things do not have to happen this way, that there is always another way, neither better nor worse, in which things might take shape. I realize in the end that I am probably powerless to affect the outcome of even the least thing that happens, but nevertheless, and in spite of myself, as if in an act of blind faith, I want to assume full responsibility. And therefore this desire, this overwhelming need, to take these papers and scatter them across the room. Or else, to go on. Or else, to begin again. Or else, to go on, as if each moment were the beginning, as if each word were the beginning of another silence, another word more silent than the last.

A few scraps of paper. A last cigarette before turning in. The snow falling endlessly in the winter night. To remain in the realm of the naked eye, as happy as I am at this moment. And if this is too much to ask, then to be granted the memory of it, a way of returning to it in the darkness of the night that will surely engulf me again. Never to be anywhere but here. And the immense journey through space that continues. Everywhere, as if each place were here. And the snow falling endlessly in the winter night.

TRANSLATIONS
1967–1969

PAUL ÉLUARD

The Lover

She is standing on my lids
And her hair is in mine
She is the form of my hands
And the color of my eyes,
She is swallowed in my shadow
Like a stone against the sky

Her eyes are always open
And she does not let me sleep
In the light of day her dreams
Make suns evaporate,
Make me laugh, cry and laugh,
And speak when I have nothing to say.

Second Nature

In honor of the dumb the blind the deaf
To the great black stone upon the shoulders
The world passing away without mystery

But also for the others who know things by their name
The burning of each metamorphosis
The unbroken chain of dawns in the skull
The persistent cries that shatter words

Furrowing the mouth furrowing the eyes
Where maddened colors diffuse the mists of waiting
Propping love against the life the dead dream of
The low-living share the others are slaves
Of love as some are slaves of freedom.

Equality of the Sexes

Your eyes have returned from an arbitrary land
Where nothing ever knew the meaning of eyes
Nor the beauty of eyes, or stones,
Or drops of water, or pearls painted on signs,

Naked stones reft of skeleton, o my statue,
The blinding sun has stolen your place in the mirror
And if it seems to obey the forces of evening
It is because your head is sealed, o my statue, beaten

By my love and savage tricks.
My motionless desire, your last support
Carried off without struggle, o my image,
Broken by my weakness and taken in my chains.

The Deaf and the Blind

Do we reach the sea with clocks
In our pockets, with the noise of the sea
In the sea, or are we the carriers
Of a purer and more silent water?

The water rubbing against our hands sharpens knives.
The warriors have found their weapons in the waves
And the sound of their blows is like
The rocks that smash the boats at night.

It is the storm and the thunder. Why not the silence
Of the flood, for we have dreamt within us
Space for the greatest silence and we breathe
Like the wind over terrible seas, like the wind

That creeps slowly over every horizon.

ANDRÉ BRETON

All Paradise Is Not Lost

The stone cocks turn to crystal
They defend the dew with battering crests
And then the charming flash of lightning
Strikes the banner of ruins
The sand is no more than a phosphorescent clock
Murmuring midnight
Through the arms of a forgotten woman
No shelter revolving in the fields
Is prepared for Heaven's attacks and retreats
It is here
The house and its hard blue temples bathe in the night
                              that draws my images
Heads of hair, heads of hair
Evil gathers its strength quite near
But will it want us?

No Grounds for Prosecution

Art of days art of nights
The scale of wounds called Pardon
Red scale that quivers under the weight of a wing
When the snow-collared horsewomen with empty hands
Push their vaporous chariots across the meadows
I see this scale jumping madly up and down
I see the graceful ibis
Returning from the pool laced within my heart
The wheels of the charming dream and its splendid ruts
Mounting high upon the shells of their dresses
And surprise bounding wildly over the sea
Depart my darling dawn forget nothing of my life
Take these roses creeping in the mirror-well
Take every beating of every lid
Take everything down to the threads that hold the steps
     of rope and waterdrop dancers
Art of days art of nights
I stand before a distant window in a city filled with horror
Outside men with stovepipe hats follow one another at
     regular intervals
Like the rains I loved
When the weather was fine
"The Wrath of God" was the name of the cabaret I entered
     last night
It was written on the white façade in even whiter letters
But the lady sailors gliding behind the windows
Are too happy to be afraid
Never a body here always the murder without proof
Never the sky always the silence
Never freedom but for freedom

TRISTAN TZARA

Approximate Man (I)

sunday heavy lid on the boiling of blood
weekly weight squatting on its muscles
fallen within itself and found again
the bells chime for no reason and we too
chime bells for no reason and we too
will rejoice in the noise of chains
that will chime within us with the bells

what is this language that whips us as we tumble into the light
our nerves are whips in the hands of time
and doubt comes with a single colorless wing
twisting tightening shriveling inside us
like the crumpled paper of an unpacked box
gift from another age to the slithering fish of bitterness

the bells chime for no reason and we too
the eyes of fruits closely watching us
all our actions are controlled nothing is hidden
the river water has washed its bed so bare
it bears away the sweet threads of glances that have dragged
at the foot of walls licking up lives in bars
tempting the weak increasing temptation drying up ecstasies
digging to the depths of old possibilities
and unblocking the ducts of imprisoned tears
ducts enslaved by daily suffocations
glances that clutch with withered hands
the bright yield of day or the shadowy apparition
offering the anxious riches of a smile
screwed on like a flower in the buttonhole of morning
those asking for calm or lust
electric shocks vibrations jolts
adventures fires certainty or slavery

glances that have edged along discreet torments
worn the city paths paid back so many degradations with charity
following in bunches round the ribbons of water
flowing toward the seas bearing
human filth and all its mirages

the river water has washed its bed so bare
that even the light slides on the smooth wave
and falls to the bottom with the heavy shattering of stones

the bells chime for no reason and we too
cares carried with us
the inner clothes
we put on each morning
unbuttoned by night's dreaming hands
adorned with useless metal puzzles
purified in the bath of circular landscapes
in cities prepared for carnage and sacrifice
near vast expansive seas
on mountains of troubled severities
in villages of painful swagger
the hand weighing on the head
the bells chime for no reason and we too
we leave with those leaving arrive with those arriving
leave with those arriving arrive when the others leave
for no reason a bit dry a bit hard severe
bread food no more bread to accompany
the tasty song on the scale of the tongue

colors put down their weights thinking
thinking or crying or staying or eating
fruits as light as hovering smoke
thinking of the heat that weaves the word
around its kernel the dream called us

the bells chime for no reason and we too
we walk to escape the swarming roads
with a flask of landscape a single disease
a single disease sowing our death
I know I carry the song in me and I am not afraid
I carry death and if I die it is death
who will carry me in his unseen arms
fine and light like the smell of thin grass
fine and light like departure without cause
without bitterness without debts without regret without
the bells chime for no reason and we too
why seek the end of the chain that links us to the chain
chime bells for no reason and we too
we will make the broken glasses chime within us
silver coins mingling with the counterfeit
the debris of festivals breaking into laughter and storm
at whose doors the void might open
the tombs of air the mills hackling arctic bones
these festivals bearing our heads to the sky
spitting molten night upon our muscles

I speak of who speaks who is speaking I'm alone
I'm nothing but a faint noise I have several noises inside me
a crumpled noise frozen on the street tossed onto the wet
     sidewalk
at the feet of rushing men running with their deaths
round death stretching his arms
on the dial of the sun's only living hour

the night's dark breath thickens
and along my veins sailors' flutes are singing
transposed into octaves from the layers of many existences
lives are infinitely repeated down to atomic thinness
and high so high we cannot see

with these lives beside us we cannot see
the ultraviolet of so many parallel paths
those we might have taken
those that might not have led us to the world
or have led us out of it already long ago so long ago
we would have forgotten the age and the earth that would have
     sucked our flesh
salts and liquid metals limpid at the bottom of wells

I think of the heat weaving the word
around its kernel the dream called us

PHILIPPE SOUPAULT

Servitudes

Yesterday it was night
but the posters sang
the trees stretched themselves
the barber's wax statue grinned at me
Do not spit
Do not smoke
rays of sunlight in the hand you told me
there were fourteen

I invent unknown streets
new and flowering continents
the newspapers will appear tomorrow
Beware of wet paint
I shall walk naked with a cane in my hand

Georgia

I do not sleep Georgia
I hurl spears in the night Georgia
I am waiting Georgia
I am thinking Georgia
The fire is like snow Georgia
The night is my neighbor Georgia
I hear each and every noise Georgia
I see the smoke that rises and wisps away Georgia
I walk like a wolf in the shadows Georgia
I am running here is a suburban street Georgia
here is a city that is the same
and I've never seen it before Georgia
I hurry on and this is the wind Georgia
and cold and silence and fear Georgia
I escape Georgia
I am running Georgia
the clouds are low they will fall Georgia
I open my arms Georgia
I do not close my eyes Georgia
I call Georgia
I cry Georgia
I am calling Georgia
I call you Georgia
Would you come Georgia
soon Georgia
Georgia Georgia Georgia
Georgia
I do not sleep Georgia
I am waiting for you
Georgia

The Swimmer

A thousand bird calls
the horizon traces a life line
And lost vague faces whisper
in gulfs held like open arms
I am certain at last of being alone
is this North is this West
the sun humming with light
street of sky and earth
I stop to ponder once more if the summer is red
in my veins
and my shadow turns around me
clock-wise
Sleep brings me insects and reptiles
pain a grimace and falsehood
waking
I float like a lost face in the midst of an hour
without help without a word
without conviction I go down the endless steps
and go on without regret until bedtime
in the eyes of mirrors and the laughter of wind
I recognize a stranger who is me
I do not move
I wait
and shut my eyes like a lock
We will never know when the night begins
or where it ends
but that hardly matters
the negroes of Kamtchatka
will sleep beside me this evening
when fatigue rests upon my head
like a crown

At the Edge of the World

Babbling in the black street, even at the end, where
           the river shudders against the banks.
Tossed from a window—a lone cigarette-butt blooms into a star.
Again, babbling in the black street.
You loud mouths!
Thick night, unbreathable night.
A cry comes near, is almost upon us,
But fades at the moment it arrives.

Somewhere, in the world, at the foot of a slope,
A deserter is talking to sentinels who do not understand
           his language.

I Have Dreamed of
You So Much

I have dreamed of you so much that you are no longer real.

Is there still time for me to reach your breathing body, to kiss your mouth and make your dear voice come alive again?

I have dreamed of you so much that my arms, grown used to being crossed on my chest as I hugged your shadow, would perhaps not bend to the shape of your body.

For faced with the real form of what has haunted me and governed me for so many days and years, I would surely become a shadow.

O scales of feeling.

I have dreamed of you so much that surely there is no more time for me to wake up. I sleep on my feet, prey to all the forms of life and love, and you, the only one who counts for me today, I can no more touch your face and lips than touch the lips and face of some passerby.

I have dreamed of you so much, have walked so much, talked so much, slept so much with your phantom, that perhaps the only thing left for me is to become a phantom among phantoms, a shadow a hundred times more shadow than the shadow that moves and goes on moving, brightly, over the sundial of your life.

Like a Hand at the
Moment of Death

Like a hand at the moment of death the shipwreck
looms like rays of drowsing sun; from all directions your
glances have aged.

There is no longer time, there is no longer time,
perhaps, to see me.

But the leaf that falls and the wheel that turns
will tell you that nothing on this earth ever lasts.

Except love.

And I want to convince myself of it.

Life-boats painted red,

Storms that flee,

An old-fashioned waltz that bears wind and weather
across long spaces of sky.

Countrysides.

I only want the embrace I yearn for,

And the rooster's song is dying.

Like the clenching of a hand at the moment of death,
my heart contracts.

Since I've known you I have never cried.

I love my love too much to cry.

You will cry at my grave,

Or I at yours.

It will never be too late.

I'll tell a lie. I'll say you were my mistress

For it's all so futile,

You and I, we'll soon be dead.

RENÉ CHAR

Lacenaire's Hand

Worlds of eloquence have been lost.

The Violent Rose

Eye in a trance silent mirror
As I approach I depart
Buoy in the battlements

Head against head to forget all
Until the shoulder butts the heart
The violent rose
Of ruined and transcendent lovers.

Poets

The sadness of illiterates in the darkness of bottles
The blind unrest of wheelwrights
Coins in the sunken vase

In the core of the anvil
The solitary poet lives
Vast wheelbarrow of swamps.

The Fired Schoolteacher

Three characters of proven banality accost one another with diverse poetical phrases (got a match, I beg of you, what time is it, how many leagues to the next town?), in an indifferent countryside and engage in a conversation whose echoes will never reach us. Before you is the twenty-acre field: I am its worker, its secret blood, its catastrophic stone. I leave you nothing to think.

Chain

The great pyre of alliances
Beneath the spiral sky of failure
In the rotted boat it is winter
From solid companions to liquid partners
Deathbeds below the crust
In the earth's vacant depths
The arcs forge a new number of wings
The bright tillage worships the sodden healers
On the straw of fatalists
The lighted star-foam flows
There is no absence that cannot be replaced.

Observers and Dreamers

to Maurice Blanchard

Before rejoining the nomads
The seducers ignite columns of gas
To dramatize the harvest

Poetic toil will begin tomorrow
Preceded by the cycle of voluntary death
The reign of darkness oozing the diamond into the mine

Mothers smitten with patrons of the last sigh
Excessive mothers
Endlessly furrowing the massive heart
Endless prey to the shuddering ferns of embalmed thighs
You will be won
You will go to bed

Alone at river-windows
Great lighted faces
Dream there is nothing that dies
In their carnivorous landscape.

ANDRÉ DU BOUCHET

The White Motor

I
I quickly removed
this sort of arbitrary bandage

I found myself
free
and without hope

like knotted sticks
or stone

I radiate

with the heat of stone

which resembles the cold
against the body of the field

but I know the heat and cold

the frame of the fire

the fire

in which I see
the head

the white limbs.

II

At several points the fire pierces the sky, the deaf side, which I have never seen.

The sky that heaves a bit above the earth. The black brow. I don't know if I am here or there,

in the air or in a rut. They are scraps of air, which I crush like clumps of earth.

My life stops with the wall, or begins to walk where the wall stops, in the shattered sky. I do not stop.

III

My telling will be the black branch that forms an elbow in the sky.

IV

Here, its white mouth opens. There, it defends itself along the whole line, with these entrenched trees, these black beings. There again, it takes the hot, heavy form of fatigue, like limbs of earth, scorched by a plow.

I stop at the edge of my breath, as if beside a door, to listen to its cry.

Here, outside, a hand is upon us, a cold, heavy sea, as if, as the stones walk, we were walking with stones.

V
I go out
inside the room

as if outside

among the still
furnishings

in the shuddering heat

alone

outside its fire

there is not yet
anything

the wind.

VI
I walk, joined with fire, in the uncertain paper, mingled with
air, the unprimed earth. I lend my arm to the wind.

I go no farther than my paper. Far before me, it fills a ravine.
A bit farther, in the field, we are almost level. Half knee-deep
in stones.

Nearby they speak of wounds, of a tree. I see myself in what
they speak. That I not be mad. That my eyes not become as
weak as the earth.

VII
I am in the field
like a drop of water
on a red-hot iron

the field itself
eclipsed

the stones open

like a stack of plates
held
in the arms

when evening breathes

I stay
with these cold white plates

as if I held the earth
itself

in my arms.

VIII
Already the spiders are running over me, on the dismembered
earth. I rise above the plowing, on the clipped and arid runnels,
                                        of a finished field, now
blue, where I walk without ease.

IX

Nothing satisfies me. I satisfy nothing. The bellowing fire will be the fruit of that day, on the fusing road, reaching whiteness in the battered eyes of stones.

X

I brake to see the vacant field, the sky above the wall. Between air and stone, I enter an unwalled field. I feel the skin of the air, and yet we remain divided.

Beyond us, there no fire.

XI

A large white page, palpitating in the ruined light, lasts until we get closer to one another.

XII

In releasing the warm door, the iron knob, I find myself before a noise that has no end, a tractor. I touch the base of a gnarled bed. I do not begin. I have always lived. I see the stones more clearly. The enclosing shadow, the earth's red shadow on my fingers, in its weakness, beneath its draping, which the heat has not hidden from us.

XIII

This fire, like a smoother wall, built on top of another, and struck, violently, up to its peak, where it blinds us, like a wall I do not allow to petrify.

The earth lifts its harsh head.

The fire, like an open hand, which I no longer wish to name. If reality has come between us, like a wedge, and divided us, it was because I was too close to this heat, to this fire.

XIV

So, you have seen these burstings of the wind, these great discs of broken bread, in this brown country, like a hammer out of its matrix that swims against the unrippled current, of which nothing can be seen but the gnarled bed, the road.

These keening bursts, these great blades, left by the wind.

The raised stone, the grass on its knees. What I don't know of the back and profile, since the moment of soundlessness: you, like the night.

You recede.

This unharnessed fire, this unconsumed fire, igniting us, like a tree, along the slope.

XV

What remains after the fire are disqualified stones, frigid stones, the change of ashes in the field.

The carriage of the foam still remains, rattling, as if it had rushed forth again from the tree, anchored to the earth with broken nails, this head, that emerges and falls into place, and the silence that claims us, like a vast field.

JACQUES DUPIN

Mineral Kingdom

In this country lightning quickens stone.

On the peaks that dominate the gorges
Ruined towers rise up
Like the nimble torches of the mind
That revive the nights of high wind
The instinct of death in the quarryman's blood.

Every granite vein
Will unravel in his eyes.

The fire that will never be cured of us.
The fire that speaks our language.

Thirst

I summon the landslide
(In its clarity you are naked)
And the dismemberment of the book
Among the uprooting of stones.

I sleep so the blood your torture lacks
Will struggle with scents, the gorse, the torrent
Of my enemy mountain.

I walk endlessly.

I walk to alter something pure,
This blind bird upon my fist
Or this too clear face, glimpsed
At a stone's throw

I write to bury my gold,
To close your eyes.

My body, you will not fill the ditch
That I am digging, that I deepen each night.

Like a wild boar caught in the underbrush
You leap, you struggle.

Does the vine on the rampart remember another body
Prostrate on the keyboard of the void?

Throw off your clothes, throw away your food,
Diviner of water, hunter of lowly light.

The sliding of the hill
Will overflow the false depth,
The secret excavation underfoot.

Calm wriggles into the night air
Through disjointed stones and the riddled heart

At the instant you disappear,
Like a splinter in the sea.

Opened in few words
as if by an eddy, in some wall,
an embrasure, not even a window

to hold at arm's length
this night country where the path is lost

at the limit of strength a naked word

The wave of limestone and the white of wind
cross the sleeper's chest

whose flooded nerves are shaking below
propping the gardens in tiers
parting the thorns and prolonging
the harmonies of nocturnal instruments
toward comprehension of the light
—and its breaking

his forked passion on the anvil
he breathes
like thunder
without food without venom among the junipers
on the slope, and the ravine makes him breathe
a dark air
to compensate for the violence of his chains

Let us salute what delivers us, the flame yellow bulldozer, the giant beetle with fever-shaken thorax, the small of its back twisted for a monstrous arching. It has come to uproot the palace and its ruins, to overturn images and stone, to fold up the domes and dovecots, to rip out the old erectile passions of men, their vertical syntax, and last of all, the prison, all that remains of the city. From now on, a clearing free from all dis-eased shadow. Bare table. A table adorned for a feast without food, without guests. I salute its enraged candor, preparing to redeem our waiting, to sign our work.

It is then that I see you grow, star. That I see you grow and shine in my tiny hand, a stone, girded against famine.

Gripped by the dread of the untold
story

the sun
the meaning
of giving in

aphasiac hub
your kingdom
since the wheel crushed me
I have denied it

Whatever the putrid smell of new neighborhoods
the instruments of decline spread out at our feet

we devour the slag
what is written without us
downwards

abrasion and aroma
contiguous and discordant
what is written obliquely and with cunning
building calm

like pyramid on its point

NOTES FROM
A COMPOSITION
BOOK
1967

1

The world is in my head. My body is in the world.

2

The world is my idea. I am the world. The world is your idea.
You are the world. My world and your world are not the same.

3

There is no world except the human world. (By *human* I mean
everything that can be seen, felt, heard, thought, and imag-
ined.)

4

The world has no objective existence. It exists only insofar as
we are able to perceive it. And our perceptions are necessarily
limited. Which means that the world has a limit, that it stops
somewhere. But where it stops for me is not necessarily where
it stops for you.

5

No theory of art (if it is possible) can be divorced from a theory
of human perception.

6

But not only are our perceptions limited, language (our means of expressing those perceptions) is also limited.

7

Language is not experience. It is a means of organizing experience.

8

What, then, is the experience of language? It gives us the world and takes it away from us. In the same breath.

9

The fall of man is not a question of sin, transgression, or moral turpitude. It is a question of language conquering experience: the fall of the world into the word, experience descending from the eye to the mouth. A distance of about three inches.

10

The eye sees the world in flux. The word is an attempt to arrest the flow, to stabilize it. And yet we persist in trying to translate experience into language. Hence poetry, hence the utterances of daily life. This is the faith that prevents universal despair— and also causes it.

11

Art is the *mirror of man's wit* (Marlowe). The mirror image is apt—and breakable. Shatter the mirror and rearrange the pieces. The result will still be a reflection of something. Any combination is possible, any number of pieces may be left out. The only requirement is that at least one fragment remain. In *Hamlet*, holding the mirror up to nature amounts to the same thing as Marlowe's formulation—once the above arguments have been understood. For all things in nature are human, even if nature itself is not. (We could not exist if the world were not our idea.) In other words, no matter what the circumstances (ancient or modern, Classical or Romantic), art is a product of the human mind. (The human mimed.)

12

Faith in the word is what I call Classical. Doubt in the word is what I call Romantic. The Classicist believes in the future. The Romantic knows that he will be disappointed, that his desires will never be fulfilled. For he believes that the world is ineffable, beyond the grasp of words.

13

To feel estranged from language is to lose your own body. When words fail you, you dissolve into an image of nothingness. You disappear.